Psychic Party Under the Bottle Tree

Jennifer Martelli

LILY POETRY REVIEW BOOKS

Additional praise for Jennifer Martelli's poetry

My Tarantella

I love this book with its strength and riskiness, its weaving of the Kitty Genovese story with the narrator's own story and life. The details Martelli provides seem so real, so rooted, so perfect for these two intertwined tales . . . This is a book I won't soon forget. Certainly, it's a book not to be missed.

—Maria Mazziotti Gillan, American Book Award winner

This collection shines its eerie and gorgeous light, filling the shadows with tarot readings for Genovese, artichoke leaves hiding secret gifts, and a whole history recast from the shimmering margins. This collection is so painfully exquisite, "It hurts my hoarse throat, my blue heart."

—Jenn Givhan, author of *Girl with Death Mask*

The Queen of Queens

This is a powerful account of past and present, strung like the book's frequently recurring pearls—symbol of femininity but also proof that a source of struggle can generate uncommon beauty. I will return to these translucent poems again and again.

—Jennifer Militello, author of *The Pact*

In complex, intelligent poems that are not afraid to grapple with difficult topics, including misogynist rhetoric from other women, Martelli has answered her own question, "how do we survive sadness?" Martelli writes about it—all the secrets and mistakes. All the false hopes and struggles. She makes bold art from history and we, her readers, are the wiser for it.

—Jennifer Franklin, author of *No Small Gift*

All Things Are Born to Change Their Shapes

I've long admired Jennifer Martelli's poetry, not just her individual poems and her original voice, but also the way she organizes her books into a cohesive whole by weaving repeating imagery and themes throughout each collection.

—Kathleen Aguero, *Solstice Lit Mag*

Copyright © 2024 by Jennifer Martelli
Published by Lily Poetry Review Books
223 Winter Street
Whitman, MA 02382

https://lilypoetryreview.blog/

ISBN: 978-1-957755-42-7

All rights reserved. Published in the United States by Lily Poetry Review Books. Library of Congress Control Number: 2024937076

Many times in our recovery, the old ghosts will haunt us.

—Narcotics Anonymous, *The Blue Book*

Table of Contents

I

- 1   *Is there anything under that layer?*
- 2   Dr. Martens 1460 Wild Botanica
- 3   Ceruse
- 4   August
- 6   Blur
- 7   400 Calories of Existential Horror
- 9   Ghostwriter
- 10   The Way This Acela Train Eats
- 11   Tarot in a Nicotine Dream
- 12   The Lens
- 13   The Structure of Milk
- 15   Rooms
- 16   Yesterday, I Dug All My Sadnesses Out of Their Storage Boxes, and Today It Snowed
- 17   My Friend Can Grow Anything in Her Backyard
- 18   Possum Haibun
- 19   Psychic Party Under the Bottle Tree
- 21   Luna Maria
- 22   Moon Jellyfish
- 23   One Year After My Friend Posted a Photo of Jean-Léon Gérôme's The Bacchante: Head of a Woman With the Horns of a Ram
- 24   I Find Relationships Exhausting
- 25   Night Snake

II

- 29   *Bysedd y cŵn,* Foxglove
- 30   The Coleus on Good Friday
- 31   I Address My Catho-alcoholism
- 32   Double Yolk
- 33   Bible Bread
- 34   Oloid
- 35   St. Cocaine of Lines, St. Anisette, St. Marijuana, St. Horse
- 37   Waiting for My Son at Midnight by the Church at the Edge of the Small Woods Where the Kids Get Stoned

38	Listening to Nicolle Wallace and Thinking of Jericho Brown's Poem
39	Stone-colored Birds
40	Sobriety
41	I Crocheted a Uterus, But Not Because I Tried
42	I Hear About Couples in America While Stuck on the Massachusetts Turnpike
43	Did it take long to find me?
44	Vision Test in the First Grade
45	Contemplating Vegetarianism
47	Dear Tortoiseshell Bowl I Stole
48	The Memory Floor
49	The Hunter
	III
53	Meat
54	Snakes
55	Watching a Re-enactment of Dick Cheney's Heart Transplant
56	The Love Between Trees is an Adult Love
57	Growing Out My Bangs
58	Someday, I Shall Love Emily Dickinson's Poems
59	Lunaria
60	Bryant Park Farmers' Market
61	Raising My Son in the Time of Pence
62	Cremains
63	Rilke
64	*Hot Things to Me Are Not Dark*
65	Fascism
66	O
67	Phoebe
68	The Chain
69	Sandy's Electric Griddle
70	Metamorphosis
71	Corinthians 13:11
72	Blades
74	*Notes*
77	*Acknowledgements*

ix

I

a green garden snake moves in the dirt,
like a question 'will you be sad tomorrow?'

—Gloria Monaghan, "The Field"

Is there anything under that layer?

I fear suffocation and I fear snakes and once,
in a movie, I saw a man with a python wrapped
around his whole head—he couldn't even scream.

That actor, a pale flaccid man, wry and always
amused, died not long ago. One summer,
the previews and teasers ran in a loop for

The Mummy redux: a young princess, betrayed
by her father, was mummified alive, wrapped in cloth
and locked in an iron tomb carved with the face

of a screaming woman and snakes. A snake
can crawl brand new out of its own long skin.
The father betrayed his daughter because he adhered

to his own mythology, like most fathers. I think I fear
suffocation because of the weight covering me, stars
asphyxiating themselves, colors imploding into

jewel-tone hues, like the diamonds of a hungry snake.
One friend insisted I fear snakes because I fear
the penis. Another said I fear trains crossing bridges

because they look like snakes if I could see them
while flying, way up where the air is too thin to breathe.
I fear suffocation and snakes and bridges and the penis,

but mostly I don't want to be disregarded. That's the fear.
I'm wrapped in snakeskin and cloth and cold, thick
iron: it's heavy, and I'm left, I'm just left.

Dr. Martens 1460 Wild Botanica

What I want is that 8-eye boot with Goodyear welt lines on the sole.
I want the Backhand black leather and the overgrown wild flower print,
and all that pink and green flora and fauna. These boots dig in, webbed
all over with Datura, Poppy, Japanese Anemone, Poison Ivy, Foxglove.
And then the things that feed and crawl and fly: moth, scorpion, black
widow, wasp. I'd switch out the factory laces with loden green: a corset
going up each foot to the ankle. I want the criss-cross to show. Sometimes,
I want to smoke again and feel that hot toxin sting the bony roof of my mouth.

But I made a vow to never again buy leather: I'd love not to harm
any living thing though I still eat fat shrimp all curled over as if in pain,
the sunny yolk inside a warm brown egg. I'll buy eggs just to paint them.
I'll smoke bees out of a hive to make honey and wax to burn down all night.
I'll call the meat of a cow *flesh* just to ruin your meal. Here is the truth of these boots:
I want you to think they're pretty, get close to me, believe me when I say I'm good.

Ceruse

The *Globe's* horoscope tells me to avoid abstract concepts,
to avoid half-truths, to change my hair, to examine
asexuality. The moon will rise at 4:09 p.m. today. A crown

of autumnal planets will have risen by then, too. I watch the end
of *Elizabeth*, when Cate Blanchett has her ladies-
in-waiting shear her hair to the scalp, all bald, paint her

with lead. *Kat*, she says to the weeping girl, *I am a virgin
again.* It took time to do this: the scissors dull,
the toxic lead and vinegar to make

ceruse, crushed with a pestle in a stone
cup. The *Globe's* horoscope warns me,
hunker down. I have all this time to watch

my plants dry up: the vines with the old nightshades
in pots out back, the mums and cosmos,
even my one succulent. I had the *idea*

of growing things. My lucky rubber plant's skeleton
is showing its leaves, bone-light
green and lunar. Someone out there is angry with me.

My horoscope says tonight, the moon isn't good:
don't reciprocate, don't reply to correspondence.

August

I confess to you now, I spy on the people I believe

rejected me. Which means, I spy on the whole world,

the whole almost-autumn sky: Cassiopeia,

The Water Jar, The White Rose Cluster.

Once, I dreamt I wore a gold silk and velvet

Delicious apple costume. It felt so warm on my skin

while I dangled from a low tree and watched

a party I hadn't been invited to.

I sent forth a swarm of late-summer electronic bees,

gold-plated with fake onyx stripes—

The stem broke and I fell, bruising my flat shoulder blades.

The smell of wine filled the whole night.

When I woke, I decided to spend too much on a knife

with a good German blade

to slice the onion I'd pulled from the scalp

of the forgiving earth.

I was meant to slice its heart core

and so I did, and there I was,

untethered, hovering above the late

summer garden.

Blur

I'm letting my lavender impatiens die
slowly in their steel boxes and clay pots—
I don't want to care for them

on the cusp of fall. I don't want to watch
their long deaths, either. My cat Maria
can't abide my leaving her even for an hour,

will look me in the eye and shit on my bed.
I learned today that not all people can blur things
with their eyes—they must look and look until

they cry or look away. I bring my white spread
to Sunshine Express Laundry, watch the spin,
the spiral. My mother told me lies about so much.

She told me my face could freeze: a grimace, a pout,
cross-eyes. She feared dirt and poverty, feared our clothes
touching someone else's. I'd planted impatiens

too shallow: all the roots exposed, thick, snake-
like. I can still let in the tiniest bit of light.
See? It's fading into fall, sooner each day.

400 Calories of Existential Horror

take up less room in my belly than
400 calories of barn owls. 400 calories

of fresh raw vegetables fill me,
but it's mostly water and roughage.

400 calories of swords—my friend
chooses to fill up on swords which is why

she still bleeds. I am always hungry!
I read that every good story is a witch's hat—

the rising action climbs the black silk
to the point, then slides down

to the ever-widening brim, the rings
of Saturn over an old lady's brow.

400 calories of raw meat
leave less room than that same amount

of oil (sesame, olive, canola, sweat), less
than *The Scream* by Edvard Munch

if I could swallow that like a secret
love letter. And another friend insists

trauma rides through her bloodstream
in bone marrow canoes. She says old

pain shapes us: drooping right eye,
inverted spine, loose uterus. 400 calories

of horror served up on stoneware

microwaveable dishwasher safe plates.

I read that every good poem
is a Rodney Dangerfield joke.

400 calories of chicken—skin on,
bone in (full and savory) is less than

400 calories of math. The stomach
is bigger than the heart, grows

like a womb, as much as it needs.

Ghostwriter

That last hot day of fall, I watched my daughter finally turn

away and look through the fogged backseat window of my car

while two friends buckled in next to her told secrets,

one little wet mouth cupped to a tender ear.

My hands at ten-til-two, my eyes on each girl, reversed

in the rearview mirror, all of us quiet, I idled the car

near the school, at the dead end of Ida Road. Last night's lightning storm

flooded most of the street, sewers overflowed,

winds downed the maples, spilled their innards, and the wires: some live

like snakes still dangerous though dead. The car's leather

seats were dark, oxblood, and soaked

in expelled heat from all of us. It smelled of rubber and something

electric, corroded. My daughter breathed on the window to make

even more fog: drew things with her finger: hearts, stars, her name.

The Way This Acela Train Eats

I watch a video on my iPhone of a python swallowing a brown fawn whole. The snake's jaws unhinge and it moves down the length of the baby deer, slides with its reticulated muscle, the way this Acela train eats the tracks through Connecticut: one smooth forward swallow. The herpetologist who narrates says the snake will have to lie with its long full body for quite a while: the shape of the fawn slowly dissolving over days, maybe a month, for the snake's juices to break down the meat so it can shit bone bits, antler buds, flat teeth, and velvet. Until then, the snake can't move at all. This is when the snake is happiest, most vulnerable and sated. I am midway between New York City and Boston—the night sky follows this last train out of the station. I drink a cold ginger ale to calm my stomach. My insides are confused: I'm sitting still and enclosed, rushing in some direction. The thin moon in each window of this train.

Tarot in a Nicotine Dream

Last night I tried to smoke under a stone
bridge. My cold hands shook, broke

each cigarette. I drew three oxidized cups
from the Tarot deck, cried,

afraid of the envy. Then I pulled the hangman
reversed. From my angle, he danced a jig

or pirouette, loose leg bent
at the knee: lack of sacrifice. The world

slowed down, no momentum from the noose
around his ankle: this pivot felt the most

practiced and careful. My friend
was there too, wearing black slacks

velvet with tiny skulls
sewn all over in white thread. I hoped

the cups meant three uteri: upside down,
they spilled rust and

patina, poison, too unsafe
to use. I tamped one cigarette end

hard against my thigh, and smoked
planning my lie, tobacco on the tip

of my tongue. *At least it wasn't booze,* I said
to the wet stone arch. When I woke, the sun

hovered behind snow and it was midday.

The Lens

In the pocket of my cotton apron: a loose
lens from an old pair of glasses. Cool
as a beach stone and as smooth, it fit

in my palm, magnified my life line,
my heart line, focused my future.
My eyes don't constrict tight as a cervix

anymore. What else can't I see?
From my kitchen window, January 1st
looks like any other Sunday, but there are trees

lying on the sidewalk, there's silver tinsel.
I'm simmering a pot of lentils for luck,
lentils because they look like coins, lentils

weeping with sweet onions and garlic cloves
peeled off their bulbs. I can see the root
lentil seed, *lensis*, convex as a lens

and green until boiled brown. *She is old,*
old, old, she must live/another year,
and she knows it. I can barely see

into the pot to stir the soup, it's steaming
with seed and the most savory sweet heat.

The Structure of Milk

I live in fear of milk gone bad,
pour jugs of it down the drain
days before the little inky date
condemns it to sour. The gallon

in my refrigerator dies on my birthday,
which I share with Yoko Ono, John
Travolta, Toni Morrison. My husband
says bad milk turns to cheese, which

I love, and him too, still, even now.
All the diets my mother followed
had her drink milk so skim, it was
blue, a light deified breast-milk

blue. I was born on the last
day of Aquarius. I once wore a gold
charm around my neck that fell
to my breastbone: a woman

holding a jug high over her head,
pouring out fake diamonds that shone.
Her tiny metal arms could just bear
the weight of those glass chips filled

to the lip. When we cleaned out
my parents' home—after—we found
packets of powdered milk unopened
in a cabinet behind the quick oatmeal,

tins of tea, a jar of instant coffee.
Food to take to the moon. Stale food,
yes, but not turned, not bad. Remnants
of a Depression girlhood. Today,

nearing the end of Aquarius, I'm warned
not to delay, not to skip a step or a rehearsal.
Try to draw a diagram, my horoscope says.
Don't wait until the very last minute.

Rooms

My little office has two windows, and the one above my cluttered desk
looks out, east, down my street, Ruby Ave. I'm half listening to two poets
read on Zoom. They are in squares and I fill in the squares of the Sunday
crossword puzzle. Still, I'm hearing a rhythm, or their rhythms travel
the cold blue cyberspace, hit and thrum the hammer and anvil in my ear.

It stays light now, after five. The snow we had this week won't last
with the extra minutes of sun. If I walked down my street, I'd hit one pond
and then a beach. The poets talk about politics now, in conversation, in poetry.
Do politics belong in a poem? The more famous writer says she writes
what she writes, what comes to her.

The chat turns to Ana Mendieta, pushed out a window by her husband.
So, how do we mourn her? Does forgiveness belong in art? Does love?
Women wept at her art exhibit: wept like a chorus for her un-answered-for
death. I'm not saying clearly what I need to say. Outside, a small icicle
falls past my window.

Yesterday, I Dug All My Sadnesses Out of Their Storage Boxes, and Today It Snowed

Think about it: sarin gas dropped on a Syrian city.
Think about it.

I was breathing then. I am breathing now.
Maybe I was watching April

the giraffe in labor, in a special pen, away from the father, her man
who wants only to kill their child. April: all long-legs and russet

spots holding up that belly. Even April can breathe. Or maybe I am just
watching a hoax. I am watching Evolene, the gold feral cat

laboring, too. Skinny wretched thing: warm
now, she spreads her hind legs, licks

her canal to heal the hurt with her wet scent. Think about
breathing. Think about it. Think of all the videos

of animals in labor. Think about how still and big eyes get in pain:
that center of dark grows and grows and grows.

My Friend Can Grow Anything in Her Backyard

We sit on her porch and eat olives out of a jar.

The days are growing longer. Now, at five, it's still light.

Soon, she says, *the crocus and the bloodroot will bloom.*

The American anemone, too.

Just one more week for this too-warm February

and then, before we know it, the vernal equinox.

Spring is hard for me, I tell her.

I'm unhappy for no reason a lot, and anxious,

angry all the time—I drop things and break them.

The oily salt stings a small cut on my fingertip.

It's the light, she says, *and the wind. There's too much*

to see, it comes at you so fast it feels like panic.

Possum Haibun

Moon creature, she waddled past my clay pots
of sleeping English lavender, Genovese basil,

black peppermint and lemon balm. Sweet
thing not of this earth, long-tailed haibun:

I, too, don't sleep through. I prayed
for relief, I prayed my dark thoughts

desiccate: tiny seeds floating out
through my ribcage. But I'm an atheist and

this is what I got: pearl-glow, warm-
blooded nighttime carrier with an anvil

in her inner ear. She traveled across
my tiny backyard, through the white

light of my television bleeding through
the French panes. She lactates deep blue

milk, lets her babies / cling to her opalescent /
pelt warm and lunar.

Psychic Party Under the Bottle Tree

*Not poppy, nor mandragora/Shall ever medicine thee
to that sweet sleep.* —*Othello,* William Shakespeare

Iago starves in a black magnum hanging from a maple branch
over my patio. I am in a green Heineken bottle, folded up
over 30 years ago by my friend who didn't want me

to marry another. I hang above him.
A cobalt blue spring water bottle from an artesian well
in France, the bottle so beautiful we call it Mother Mary,

holds an old friend from school. There's a sparrow
who won't go near the stale bread heels on the porch.
Its body darts like the head of a snake. It should starve

before it comes close, though some bold birds peck
at the bottles hanging from the tree, hoping for suet.
Their beaks make a *ting-ting* sound that keeps us up

all through the day and at night. There's a pretty girl stuffed
in an orange glass snifter globe hanging from a plastic
fishnet. She sits on a melted candle and when she cries,

her sobs sound like glass clinking. *I'm sorry,* she says.
In the summer, we ate ice cream out of cups with flat wood
spoons. I licked the sweet chocolate and vanilla swirl so hard

I got splinters in my tongue. When we were young,
we sterilized safety pins with small flames and pierced
our numbed earlobes. The earrings dangled, too, delicious.

Tiny lights nailed onto the fence illuminate the whole yard.
The birds peck at the wires, thinking they're worms. Seeds twirl, hover
down from the maple. A psychic holds a pendulum crystal

on a string, lets it hang over the flagstones. Circles mean *yes*,
back and forth, *no*. Will we leave the bottle tree? *Yes*.
Will we leave the bottle tree soon? *No*. Will we sleep?

Ever at all? Without nightmares or dreams?

Luna Maria

I have 206 bones in my body and most
could be my friends or people I envy:

clavicle for her music; radius for her reach;
patella, my old crush; and tibia and fibula and phalanges—

actors or wise guys I grew up with. The moon is an old
skull with dried-up watery ideas, basaltic and ancient.

Here are my favorite waters of the moon: Sea
of Crises, Sea of Knowledge, Seething Bay,

Bay of the Center, Lake of Time, Lake of Fear.
The bones of an old pelvis are prayers and tonics: sacrum,

ilium, coccyx. That night in Salem I put meat
into my body for the last time, I felt as if I were drinking pure

mammal fear as I sipped hot bone marrow broth
from a lunar green bowl.

Moon Jellyfish

Walking the low tide beach at dusk, I stopped short at a dead jellyfish:

pink poison (a tattoo on the nape of a neck) still stinging, hurtful.

Further on, another: Uncle Fester's bald scalp—dumb, electrified.

Hundreds left strewn all over the mud: clear sandy blobs, half-globe sadnesses.

One jellyfish lay like a broken Magic 8 ball: too hazy to tell.

One had black sand dried into a small V, like the back of a pixie cut

or a soul patch, shaved and groomed, a mound shorn to please: sexy and so plump.

One fit into a bra, balanced breasts. One missed the wave, couldn't get home.

A heavy-set woman paddled her board towards the little harbor, north.

Did you see all of these? I yelled, my words echoed off her sunburnt skin.

One, a dried purple plum. One had the imprint of a toddler's soft arch.

The harbor illuminated with globe lights strung off the yacht clubs' piers.

I realized this was my old drunk nightmare but I wasn't sure who else knew.

The boozy boats moored, bobbing? The woman, rowing, hair pulled up and clasped?

One Year After My Friend Posted a Photo
of Jean-Léon Gérôme's *The Bacchante: Head
of a Woman With the Horns of a Ram*

a woman crawls through a hole behind her medicine cabinet,

finds an unused apartment: walls skimmed smooth,

doors hung, shelves for cups, hooks to hang

spider plants and lunaria in macramé slings

knotted with undyed cotton yarn. She could put a baby

grand piano in this living room. She could have two

living rooms! She posts this discovery to her TikTok

and the video goes viral in a single day, this dream

I've had my whole life. In the dream dictionary—the one

with a creepy-eyed sun and crescent moons against

a blue nighttime sky—it says: *dreaming you've found*

that hidden or secret room suggests new strengths,

new roles. When I wake the next day, I'll sprout thick horns

like a ram. They'll curl back into me.

I Find Relationships Exhausting

Since seven this morning, I lay in the center
of my Cali-King on sheets so high in cotton count,

they feel like butter or memory or sin.
I'm doing what the New York Times calls *languishing*

and I'll do it until noon, playing Words Without Friends on my phone,
proud I know *adz* or *qi* or *aa,* can click

the letters into square spaces that explode
the screen. I make my list of needs as well: lemons

for the zest, vanilla bean for pound cake, butter by the stick-load,
coiled balls of steel to scour pots and bowls. When we cleaned

out my parents' house, my sisters and I found silver to sell off—tea services,
butter knives shaped like swords, spoons that could conduct heat—

so much we had to fill pillowcases—the ones
my mother loved, embroidered with little forsythia buds and baby's breath.

Night Snake

I try to bend my back
to the sadness. The moon

grows back
fat, a yellow scythe. Perseus

decapitates
the head of the Gorgon, snakes

litter the cold sky, just as
dangerous dead. My friend

found one black
snake head, one rat's

tail, juniper buds
waxy and strewn in her yard

after a quiet night.
Anything I've ever feared

regenerated, came
around on the wheel St. Catherine-

like, moon-
sure, rose

from the wet
humus in my heart.

Tonight another old white man
told me bend

my back back like

a bow to the sadness.

The moon waxed
fat again, a mezzaluna dull

metal all ready for my weight.

II

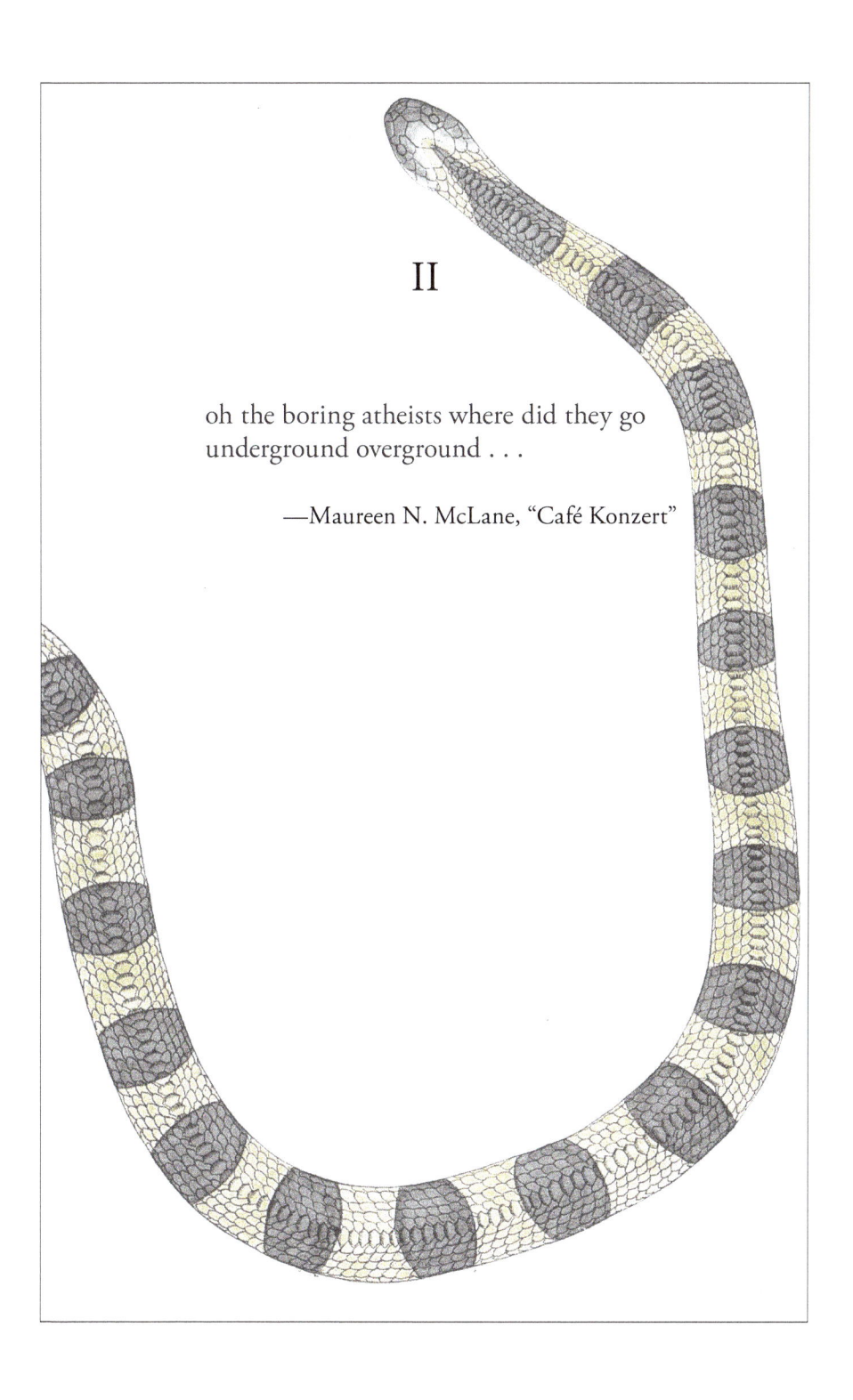

oh the boring atheists where did they go
underground overground . . .

—Maureen N. McLane, "Café Konzert"

Bysedd y cŵn, Foxglove

Do you, too, live an un-prayerful life?
Are you afraid of it, too, this un-

god? I'd like to travel to Wales,
learn that almost-outlawed tongue

of un-vowels, the Y that hangs
below the line. There is a house

called *Ty Bywyd,* Life House,
that grows out of a green meadow:

would I call it brutalist, with its brick
and glass? Yes, it is brutal. I know this house

from a movie set: its clean halls,
its heart—and it has one—bricked

and buried under a gentle rise. Is your atheism
the same as mine? Shamed and afraid?

Rules governing the letter Y are some
of the most confusing in Welsh:

can sound like my *eat,* like my *cut.* In my brick
heart of American hearts,

something moves to the edge, is built
beneath a field of foxglove.

The Coleus on Good Friday

Member of the mint family, fleshy stemmed,
tough as a fist, and thick. Those bushy hairy leaves
left in the sun turn purple, make a shallow cleft,

a warm cunt. *God, one gift*
would have been enough but he didn't stop.
Out the window, I can see where the lilies lie

awake under the thawed earth in my yard. The roots
of the word *coleus*: sheath, male part fused tight
into a fat stamen, power to stand,

stamina, and the warp
of an upright loom in ancient Rome.
I should mourn and contemplate the slow death

of a man on a cross this first mild afternoon.
I should water and dust this unwanted gift,
move the tin pot around the room for light.

I Address My Catho-alcoholism

and ask why the roots
of my hair are like the white bulbs

of tender spring onions, and is this why
I cry each equinox? Why a church

with a burning
ribcage rages in the middle of a river and what

of the thirsty churches?
Tonight,

in the mid-spring sky, the long
constellation of Queen Berenice's hair coils

over my house. And Corvus the Crow
looks for water. The Scales of Libra weigh.

I'm balancing at last, well past
my own apogee.

Double Yolk

In some folklore, cracking a double yolk egg onto a frying pan means
good fortune, the yolk yellow as gold. Buy a new egg cup! Time to plan
that baby! Time for rebirth! Change for the better or for the worse!
Time to plant a new tooth deep through the gum line to the jawbone!

Some things stop serving me but I forget to leave them behind.

Double yolk in Norway means death. Avoid double yolks in Norway.
Don't turn an egg on its head, don't invert it like a Tarot card.
Double yolk in a brown shell means it's local. Double yolk,
white shell begs to be dipped in vinegar dye.

Double yolk is Christ's dual nature: man and god. Avoid religion.

Avoid dreams of dripping yolks. Avoid dreams of breaking things.
Double yolk in a cracked egg in a dream portends a downturn,
portends potential dupled duplicity, my duality, my conflict.
But I am awake. I heat butter and salt in an iron pan until they weep.

Bible Bread

The bread I toast is so holy, they quote the Bible
to list all the ingredients: *Take also unto the wheat,
and barley, and beans, and lentils, and millet, and spelt.*

I use a hot flat knife to cleave the slices frozen and
cloven together in my freezer, where I keep sacks
of shelled edamame, the last of the summer basil pesto,

Impossible Meat. Noah's dove with an olive branch
hovers on the plastic bag: *and the dove returned to him. . .*
All the drowning was done. All the drowning

of the griffins and lutists and wolves, the women,
all done now. *Put them in one vessel, and make bread. . .*
I'd heated the knife in a saucepan of boiling water

to split the cold slices easier, pry the loaf apart. The knife
was still warm: the sunny yellow butter spread
so easily across the earth-brown grains.

Oloid

Saturday, awake to the raw April outside. A dream that was on my tongue is gone with a swallow. Blue light from the TV, from my phone.

*

Doctors say blue light interrupts the circadian system, plays a role in heart disease, cognitive dysfunctions.

*

One day, my mother couldn't remember the steps in making her bed. Which came first? The spread or the top sheet? I was impatient. Had never seen dementia. This was before I started falling asleep with the TV on. Or maybe not.

*

When I read *circadian*, I hear *cicada*. The cicada rhythm.

*

This is what happens in the spring once we pass the equinox: one day, it's light after seven at night. And look: the maples have budded, the forsythia.

*

One day, a sculptor/mathematician discovered a new shape he called the *oloid*.

*

One day, the oloid didn't exist. Next day, it did. Like a death, reversed.

*

Julie Chen, poet/artist, in her visual project, cut this shape out with a laser, splayed it on a table, folded it into a chrysalis.

*

If I believed in angels, I'd say a two-dimensional oloid looks like an angel or a winged thing. I watch Chen's process in bed, cocooned, on my phone. Beyond me, the TV is on mute (a French movie about the undead). The window is above the TV. Then the maples. Then the world.

*

One day, let me wake and feel different than I have my whole life.

*

Chen wrote: *It is the relationship of the circles that creates the shape.* The heart of the chrysalis, of the cicada, of the circadian rhythm, is a bisected, symmetrical thing, the spine of a book broke open, *dividing the coherent past/ from the incomprehensible present.*

*

All night and into the shock of day, I can hear things: wings, a humming outside, the start of rain.

St. Cocaine of Lines, St. Anisette, St. Marijuana, St. Horse

My mother owned a cauldron so rusted, nothing could live in it.

Sometimes, I swore, I could feel the sharp tips of the orange crescent moon.

Back then, my favorite Beatle was George, best color, black, best day Wednesday.

I liked to be strange and I was. But that's a lie. I'd just want and want.

And Grandma said: *wanting wanting wanting wanting wanting.*

Once, in the farms, I picked up a long willow stick and immediately

it transformed into a garter snake. Nixon was the President.

Even now, I question the symmetry of his name, the heart of cross.

In the golden church I sat tonight, I watched a sweet young girl itch—

delicious nod, her long arms like the ivory saint with the plate of eyes,

her crown of lit candles. I want to read illuminated mysteries:

I want to read about the woman saints, the drunk ones, the wrecked and wasted.

Once, in the farms near my ranch house, I dug down to rutted earth for clay.

I could mold small figures with the soft gray mud, bake them hard in the sun.

Waiting for My Son at Midnight by the Church at the Edge of the Small Woods Where the Kids Get Stoned

I suppose I should be worried:

the stained-glass windows of Our Lady Star of the Sea lit so late.

Maybe lights are tucked among the flowers that fill the moat around the church,

the new croci, queen of night tulips, impatiens.

A long time ago, I prayed for sobriety, but what I meant was

don't let me be lonely. Even when I stopped believing in God,

I prayed my kids would never feel as I do. There are some flowers

that bloom at night, moon flowers, Jessamine. Perhaps the church

is backlit inside: the windows throb like human organs: blue heart,

maroon brain, gold spleen. The little cement Mary in front of her church

was cast bent, offering her white-robed belly to the town.

Listening to Nicolle Wallace and Thinking of Jericho Brown's Poem

Today, I let my son drive home from school. It's a dangerous time,
driving west in my town, the sun lower, away from the ocean—
Pleasant Street, under an arbor of bare branches splitting and
cleaving against the blue, blue sky like old blood vessels across the sclera.
The forsythia trees—or are they bushes—too frightened to bloom
full yellow: we haven't warmed a degree. Something's wrong this year.
I slept through the equinox, past April Fool's. It's January 90th.
I'm a nervous passenger, but hide it in my right foot. I won't allow
him his Spotify while he's at the wheel so we listen to MSNBC.
The pretty anchor, the conservative, says, *Time to find your prayer beads.*
Nicolle, I've been praying for years. And here I am, my Ugged
right foot, warm in shearling, in camel suede, pressing down, in panic—
today, in the New Yorker, I read a poem that ended stressed
and masculine with the most beautiful words, *And the moon goes.*
Some things don't end hard, they go on. Every day since the false thaw
feels like 0 o'clock, the eve of St. Nothing Day.

Stone-colored Birds

I've always lived by the shore and this one has a stone circle to mark the sun
and it's surrounded by squat pink roses and sea grass, empty Seagram's.

We started giving the light back five days ago, and still the kids are in school.
The boys in my son's class made a list of ugly girls they'd dance with for a dollar.

On the walk down past the copse and the ivy wall, I saw something blue—
three stone-colored birds rose from the bush, banked left, flew off toward Dogtown.

In a pair of my daughter's jeans (washed and washed again, packed away for Goodwill),
I found old gum deep in the pocket and a tiny note folded so hard, the blue ink barely blurred:

I'm friends with mean girls and I feel like I'm drowning. The girls know who was written down.
No matter how beautiful their dresses on that hot June, don't you think the girls will know?

They'll always know and their mothers will too.

39

Sobriety

When I left today after being cruel
to my kids, I saw a black and yellow

garter snake along the footpath
behind the high school

and the temple. Its back was broke,
and when a snake breaks its back

its whole body is broke. The snake
dragged itself from one bush to the other—

the juniper not yet ginned up. I fear
snakes and I fear my children

being lonely, as I am lonely. Some men
take up snakes knotted in a wooden latch box

at the church's altar. A thirsty snake (diamond
back, copperhead) can't make venom, and so

the bites around the men's wrists
come to nothing more

than a headache. The snake on the path
looked like a slow train

at night, its cars (reading car, club and
bar car, diner) lit up,

busy. That's how it looked
anyway from my distance above.

I Crocheted a Uterus, But Not Because I Tried

Burly men hoisted the saints on their shoulders and marched them through my town.

Lucy, Anthony, Peter, Rocco, Padre Pio, the Madonna:

saints paraded through the August streets, feathered in silvery teal bills,

each bill, a prayer. Those in more pain taped bigger bills to cement robes.

Once, a distant niece was dressed as an angel, hooked to a cable, hung

over an ocean of hands. Later, my friend took a lily from church

stuck it in a glass jar on her yellow kitchen table. Cream stigma—

comical, lumpy: an old-world penis. She taught me how to crochet

one summer during the feasts. She said I needed to count, *Make sure you*

finger all your stitches and keep your loops loose so the hook goes through!

My hands grew soft as the orange yarn let go its lanolin, the steel

hook slippery. I crocheted a uterus, but not because I tried.

Look, I said, *look at the womb! It's like an old holy woolen relic!*

She brewed strong black coffee in a tin pot. We talked about our sins.

I Hear About Couples in America While Stuck on the Massachusetts Turnpike

A poet and their partner restore medieval liturgical robes.

Some vestments are embroidered with Bible stories: snakes, floods, the holy rood.

Some so old they crumble with the weight and oily poison of fingers.

Some nest and feed small white worms: the robes, big mothers lactating spit.

Stoles, copes, chimeres, tippets: purple loden green and gold silk, wine-stained.

The air is velvet pomegranate at dusk, but by moonrise, ripe plum.

Every car in front of me is turning a slow creak double-lane left.

Every tail light in front of me looks like two red lollipops, broken.

A man deep in America and his bride shoot at doomed fireflies

flashing for sexual partners on the last warm night of their bright lives.

The couple under the American sky doesn't know what glows and glows.

Every car in front of me rides with their brake lights on: someone might cross.

Nothing flies well in this wet night heat: not moths, not fat gold June bugs, not

bullets, not owls, not souls. When someone dies tonight, they'll have to wait.

Did it take long to find me?

"Moonshadow" is a happy prayerful song, a song

from Teaser and the Firecat. Long ago,

album covers were big and the Firecat

was an orange moon and the moon

was as silver as Teaser's hair. In the song,

a man is dismembered—hands, eyes,

legs, mouth, tongue, all gone, yet he remains

grateful, like Job, whose daughter Eyeshadow

is killed and is returned along with her sisters,

Cinnamon and Dove, and all Job's lands,

as a reward from God. Long ago,

I admired gratitude, prayed for pain to teach me,

until I felt pain. Now, I'm just

greedy, clumsy. In last night's dream,

I made messy cat eyes with liner,

 smudged ashy gray silk weed around

my orbital sockets. The moon

was my grandma's eye, looking down,

for me, her lids shadowed

by anemia and soft powdery blue.

Vision Test in the First Grade

When my teacher told me to place my eyes against the box,

she asked: *do you see the apple on the picnic table?*

I did see it, the apple, a ghost apple, more beautiful after its death:

glowing like a Lite Brite peg, hovering over a wooden table

which floated, too, against a black velvet campground, so shadowed

and deserted, I couldn't tell the trees apart. What if I saw,

on that same table, against the endless night in that box,

an amber pear, lit from within its skin? What if I saw a plum,

dark as that midnight picnic, but new-moon illuminated?

What would my teacher mark in her green book? As a child,

I was frightened most of the time and just bright enough.

The apple was lit from someplace else and I saw it there, boxed.

Contemplating Vegetarianism

The night the spiders fell
covering the dark windows

with their red bellies and silk
spit, I saw a tiny chamber quartet

inside the emptied ribcage
of the twenty-pound fowl

I'd boiled clean of meat for soup. The whole
kitchen smelled of rosemary

and the cellist—the only man
sitting—tuned his instrument,

but still couldn't play
the notes right: the savory warped the wood

curved it, like a woman
resting her tired self

on his chest and through
the kitchen window

above the stone sink, I saw
them fall,

the spiders, I thought it was a miracle,
I saw them fall

through the layer of gray
lace moths

who had been there all night
clinging

to the steamy glass
out in the cold

and I felt the gut strings pulled
taut by the bow's low moan.

Dear Tortoiseshell Bowl I Stole

from my father's chest of drawers, why
do you visit me in my poems? You stay
cool, cupped in my palm: a hard breast,
milkless, a moonless half-planet: marbled
whiskey gold, wine red.

I dumped my father's coins, loose buttons,
tie clip embossed with the White House,
right into the trash, blew the dust
from your hollow scoop,
filled you with the Rosaries I stole, too.

Coiled and tangled *Ave Marias:*
the onyx and sterling and light wood decades
on little knotted steel chains,
and still you're hungry.

The Memory Floor

I remember the day I stopped believing in God: October, past noon, on the Lynnway, the ocean behind the burnt-out nightclubs, the lots, behind Building 19. I was stopped in traffic, in a line of red brake lights in front of West Lynn Creamery. A milk truck—white with red letters—parked on the brick dairy's roof, odd as a ship in a bottle: did a milkman drive it up there? Did they disassemble the truck first? Was it hollow? I thought of my friend Pete, who hadn't shot dope over a decade, who hadn't fished the Grand Banks in years, who died one morning in a woman's arms. *It was dawn,* she said, *he woke up gasping and then he was gone.* My mother would live one more twilight year, my father intubated another week. Life is scary and we scare so easily. Who would design it this way? I said it out loud, *I don't believe in God. I don't believe in a plan.* I went back to wondering why this good real estate by the ocean wasn't developed into a prettier place: houses with windows that blinded you when the sun rose over Nahant. A pier. A breaker of huge gray granite rocks leading to a lighthouse. My father couldn't accept his dying. We'd sit in his hospital room, me in the chair or on the foot of his bed until he'd write, *I want out now, why don't you go.* My mother could still smile and nod at the home across town on the memory floor. Justice would have taken them first, before the tubes and straps, before my friend who left the way a dream leaves once you open your eyes. That day by the creamery, the world was turning toward Halloween. I think it was cold already. I do forget if I'd left the cosmos to die in their pots. If the geese had formed themselves into arrowheads, pointing away.

The Hunter

Such useless things, the sliding doors in my bedroom,
always drafty, opening to nothing except the overhang,
and then my neighbor's backyard and so,

when they felled the big pines and maples, I bought
thick red velvet drapes to draw closed on an iron rod
with antler finials made of amber glass. Really:

I'd been saying to my husband for years and years
we should dry wall these windows, make them smooth,
cover them with photos and macramé hangings

woven with little mirrors, feathers, eyes. One night
during a hot wet fall, around compline, I heard
wings outside, thicker than feathers or the birds

I'd hear daily. They sounded heavy,
leathery. They hovered. They left. I threw back
the drapes, hoped to see what made this glove-

slap sound. But these sliders are so foolish—
I couldn't see the bat, the moon, couldn't even trace
the constellations with my finger. Not the bear, the swan,
not the dog, not the hunter, not the cross, the keel.

III

a handwritten list of the people I love
and the mountains they've slipped from.

Each morning, I touched their names.
I picture the friend, the sister, then picture the sun.

—Eugenia Leigh, "The Mechanics of Survival"

Meat

In the dream during my second sleep,

the letters and all the words in the book

I wrote morphed: sharp glyphs

with horns, eyes laid sideways, arrows,

black birds flying away. I wake too

late on Sunday and cook meat in salty

red sauce to make amends to my husband

for my mean words I said and meant.

The sausages fry in their gut tubes,

curled, lovers spooning, and the skin

sears in fat and spices: fennel, sage,

pepper. Plath, in her journal, wrote

The letters grew barbs and rams' horns.

Shall I eat this meat after years of not?

Shall I reach out? Today, what is it

I must attend to with love?

Snakes

I have to learn to breathe differently, here,

Las Vegas-style. Today, I'll tour the Strip

and all the ways my diamondback snake

brain could unhinge and fix: blackjack, cool

green menthol cigarettes, shrimp curved

in pain on ice sculpted into the Pietá.

I ask my friend, whom I've loved

longer than my husband or my children,

about snakes. I've done my research:

colubridae, Mojave green, sidewinder,

coachwhip, panamint rattler, basin green.

Will they come to the blue warm pool

she dug out back, surrounded by brush

and cacti blooms, herbs? *No,* she said,

only baby scorpions come. Clear and small

as my fingertip, all crustacean, arachnid

and clawed. She says I may get a nosebleed

because of the heat, the arid air, the strange

elevation of a city so deep in its dry basin.

Watching a Re-enactment of Dick Cheney's Heart Transplant

There is that moment when neither has a heart:

the brain-dead boy lying on the table with his chest cracked open,

the old man with a fist-sized hole who will never know gratitude—

the good heart is handed surgeon to surgeon and hovers,

so there is a moment, much like when Sisyphus gets his stone to the top

       of the mountain and stands on the flat land

pushing nothing, he doesn't know what to do with his arms, which won't lower,

much like that moment just after the last line of cocaine is inhaled, the mirror

       licked clean,

moment of emptiness, and I'd say, *I'm OK, I've got everything I'd ever need or want.*

Even the monotonous rotation of the earth, of small moons around outer planets,

stops, and a window cracks open

letting in a strange thaw in winter. The surgeons plant a purple heart deep in old soil,

and it beats and beats and beats.

The Love Between Trees is an Adult Love

Women have limbs and so does the maple.
The tree guy climbed in her hair with his saw.

The other maples nearby entwined their branches over her,
made a canopy for privacy, let loose their chemical volatiles.

The leaves grew deep, deep green with tannin.

It was as if the trees read our lips
from their side of the fence, through our glass doors,
and knew what we had planned. They alerted each other.

Then, the willows cross town sent their sugar through the roots
to heal her exposed wound: her innards glowing white on her stumpy trunk.

She received nectar from the larch one block up
by the beach to balance her: all no-arms and lop-sided.

Even the old mottled oak who always sleeps sent forth the worms
and green moths to bind her.

Growing Out My Bangs

When I crossed Humphrey Street on my way / to the short brick row of shops—bank, dry cleaner, / deli, liquor store (everything but a place to buy rope) / I passed under the worms dangling from the maples, / and for a moment, I didn't feel afraid, / jealous, unnoticed, hungry, hot. / I heard a siren from blocks over but / couldn't tell which streets, which way, how far / and turned to see my poor old body pooled, / on the sidewalk, like a dress I'd stepped out of and left / for next morning to wash. / So I figured I was dead, had died minutes ago, but hadn't been told. / Shame. I'd worn my favorite headband, too: / the one with plastic horns: thick, pink, and pearlescent   that held fast, and shone.

Someday, I Shall Love Emily Dickinson's Poems

But until that day, I shall love her letters,
her basket full of cookies lowered

from her window by a pulley. I lay
in my bed that faces the west-facing

windows. They are high on the wall
and crank open. I can see the moon

at its apex most nights, and if I'm awake,
a single star in the morning. I vowed

to read one Dickinson letter each night,
the way I vow not to hurt myself just

for one day: no cigarette, no drink, no
gossip (hard). In 1845, Dickinson wrote,

*Dear A.____ with what delight shall I
witness their suspense.* I saw a photo

of three dancers in mid-leap or mid-land
hovering above a golden honey-oak floor,

their round calf muscles, their curved
arches, their hands tense and splayed

like stars. How I love the arabesque
or the fist that never lands, the moon

stuck in my window, a letter stolen
from or never sent to the beloved.

Lunaria

But sadness had already found me, up past Brockport, by the Erie Canal
on a road with thin treelings wrapped in white cloth for the April Fool's frost and
over a metal bridge, past ranch homes with no basements: aqua, dull pink, and brown.

Later, in that long upstate dusk, I heard
soft worn leather ballet slippers squeak on mellow wood with each foutte,
each rotation on the toe. The Earth rotates, and I think the moon circles me too.

On the news, before bed at the Hampton Inn on Lake Ave., my favorite anchor
said the threads tethering us to hope have grown more gossamer, and
I thought of lunaria seeds from the money plant, those silk silver dollars

plucked from a garden, dried and translucent—
        my mind, too, like the gossamer moon: magnetic and circular and rawbone.

Bryant Park Farmers' Market

I wouldn't mind missing the fast train home.
I'll stay with the woman sitting by the baskets of Anjou and Bosc pears:

she smudged her house with smoking sage to cleanse it,
and yet, had to flee.
Two Russian Blues play at her feet, eat from a can.

She's named them both Smokey: they are brothers.
Gentle brother Smokey. Green-eyed Smokey.

The produce here is gold, and there is lavender.
Bins of gold winter fruit. Lavender, dried and
sober. I want to stay here, folded, shameless.

Raising My Son in the Time of Pence

The beach grass bends
left: I see the blades' underbellies, beige below

green. Back when my son was born, an artist carved
half-moons into nine tall gray stones

circling a bronze sundial up here, beyond the dunes
and the roses on the crushed rocks. Four boys

I don't know kick a hacky-sack back
and forth on their bare tender high arches:

they play within the long
shadows of the stone circle—their chests

tattooed blue
by the moving light. No one can cross

through their game, break
the arcs. No one.

Cremains

I make my squirrels fat, feed them oatmeal apple bars, bread

slathered with almond butter. My last living cat likes to watch

them scurry down from the maple in my neighbor's yard, likes

to watch them on the patio bricks and her eyes become moons.

Upstairs, in my bedroom which rests in the middle branches,

I keep three small oak boxes filled with cremains. Good kitty,

good kitty, good kitty. The boxes remind me of the hope chest

samples they gave us back in high school: little coffins to fit a doll.

I've been sober over thirty years, more than half my life spent dry

as a god's unused flute. If I opened up a hole in my skin, filled that hole

with anything, my heart would explode.

Rilke

Long ago, my dinner plates were thick glass that shone green in a certain light.

They were fired with white spirals, like frost across a windshield.

I forced my friends to listen to me at my kitchen table, made longer with fold-out wings.

I read Rilke's poem about the angel who wrestles Jacob until he lay sore, still.

Back then, we had angels like John Travolta and Nic Cage, wings furled under coats.

The angels smoked, went into heat, fell in love, fell from heaven, left swirls of feathers.

They envied us, with all our hungers, our death.

We wanted to believe that our suffering was enviable, graceful, necessary.

I served my friends cold grapes, raw fish, pepper salad. Read my Rilke.

I can't remember which translation, though.

Bly's: *this is how he grows, by being defeated decisively by constantly greater beings.*

Snow's: *his growth is: to be deeply defeated by ever-greater beings.*

I can't speak for fidelity to another language or another life.

Fall lasts long past the equinox: it spirals out into the night.

Hot Things to Me Are Not Dark

—Nurse Wolf, Dominatrix

I saw her on *Donahue* in the '90s, began my slow transformation

into a blotched cow, learned to line dance on the molecular level: this is how

I recovered from self-injury, from being a girl-child among girl-children.

When I had my daughter, my fears were lonely: I unzipped them

as if they were cattails by the pond where the snakes go. Unzipped their whole

velvet torsos, their tight girdles, let loose fear fear fear into the warm autumn sky.

Tonight, the gray moths stay stone still as angel hearts all night on my screen door,

gush dumb tragedy from their arterial wings. The moths are collective: come

as one thought to their deaths at the porch light.

Fascism

So now I have Venmo and no use for credit cards. I can't even chop
my sadness into powder on the long edge of debt. I lost the milk glass
cake dish, the one with a fluted stand, the one shaped like a little woman
with a big brim hat. I can't draw out my sadness on its surface. I don't
even carry bills to roll into a straw. I don't own straws. I shave with a cartridge—
no straight-edge razor to slit an eye-hole and pull a red satin dress through—
all empire-waisted and bell-sleeved. My daughter dances on Instagram:
her red silk camisole, her velvet wine leggings make her a single intention,
a thick lip-sticked mouth moving through her tiny Park Slope apartment.
She dangles mirrors from her ceiling to make it bigger, balances bowls
of water on her bed table, her bureau drawer, the back of a lavender book
to capture more light than she'll ever need. She films through a prism,
her iPhone on a tripod, moves to Liz Phair, Björk on Spotify: songs sung
before she was born. She says that I still shave my legs smooth because of fascism.
You don't even know how bad it's pulled you to the right and then she laughs.

O

My son Michael grows into his German Shepherd

hands. Last night, he cupped a bowl of bone broth, asked

about death. *It's all the same,* Vin said, *when we die*

it shouldn't change the relationship. I hated him

at the trendy new restaurant in Salem, hated him on the way home,

hated only as a wife can, and so I asked if he ever once

practiced introspection, ever once phoned a friend who was dead.

Well, I talk to you. His eyes were so level: amber tortoise-shell cups

I took from my parents' house—after—when we cleaned it out

to sell. How could I stay mad? How could I not fill those cups

with clips, loose beads, a mottled stone?

Phoebe

says, *I was up in the room by the trees making my girl's bed and I could still smell her sleep. When I snapped the sheet, starlings, ten thousand it seemed, rose from the old larch all at once, settled, rose again and flew off. And then I lay down. But only my body slept, something else was awake but trapped.* The bowl on my table is filled with blood oranges which, during Advent, are un-gassed green and sweet and five for a dollar. I peel a section off my own (it sighs like a red bird's lung) and offer it to her. She takes my hand. *I've given over all the easy things—the envy and greed, but not what I love: my daughter, my life. How do I do that? Let go of what I love?* She opens her palm and points to the crescents etched on the seams with her gibbous moon fingers. *Don't tell anybody this. It's mine.*

The Chain

Tucked in the toe of an odd sock, my lost
silver chain lies curled and knotted too tight
to fit around my neck even as a choker, some links

broken like an old snake's cervical bones. Once,
I wore it strung with a silver charm, a horn, that fell
to my throat's hollow, kept away the curse

of eyes and of envy. Today is the coldest day
so far this year. I've hung straw crosses
from backdoor posts for St. Brigid, patron saint

of abortions and things thawing: deep dirt
pockets of animals and roots: snakes and last year's
roses, sleeping voles. I can unknot this chain

with two sharp common pins, pick the tiny locked
spine, loosen all the archaic root words of *chaine*:
links of precious metals or of iron; to twist, to twine,

to hunt, to snare. *Jealousy can open the blood,*
It can make black roses. I can wound badly and
I have. Today, I enter my daughter's birth month

and my own. *You are metal,* my chart says,
you attract and you orbit: beware toxic loops.

Sandy's Electric Griddle

Once, at a meeting in the golden basement
of St. James Catholic Church, my friend Sandy shared
he believed we're always moving forward, even,
he said, *if we use again, we're still going in the right direction.*

Do you believe you have a soul? Do you believe it's always moving forward?

Sandy loved (in no order I'm aware of): his brass alto
saxophone, ballet, astronomy, he loved being clean,
mean women.

                    Before he left to die,
he stopped by my house, asked if he could store an electric griddle,
here, in my basement. We smoked and I said

*don't leave, Sandy, stay here where we love you
and can help.*

                Do you think I'm foolish? To cling to and hide this scratched thing?

After his funeral, his ex-girlfriend called me for the griddle: I lied,
said I'd gave it away to someone who needed it, gave it away for free.

Metamorphosis

As I walked the causeway along the beach to Little Nahant,
a man came toward me with a giant spool of orange waxy twine.

He let it unspool between his hands, tied it to stakes
along the sea grass and beach plums to slow down erosion on these rooted dunes.

I waved, not to him, but to Sylvia Plath's Egg Rock and bean-green Atlantic,
waved to all her anger and vengeance and joy. I would love this man's job.

If I could unspool, and save something, I'd walk in my new clogs, the gold ones
with wings, and insist I was a minor god who granted mercies and limits.

I'd unspool the length of a life, smooth it out, cut it with the long shears
dangling from my waist. I'd tell you to burn nutmeg and pennyroyal and rue.

I'm the god they find deep in the caves, etched next to owls—
I'm the big-eyed one. I'm the figure dug up from a ruin, my holes made with sticks.

I'm the one lying across the curve of a chipped clay bowl used to catch wine or blood:
see? the crude outline of my spool? the wings at my feet? my long blades?

Corinthians 13:11

I follow Marcia Brady on Twitter: Mo McCormick, Actor/Author.

She posts a video with her older brother and they dance, a fast waltz,

under an oak tree with dozens of hanging pastel paper parasols.

She holds his hands, looks up into his face: he watches her feet.

I wish we were friends. I'd call her, Mo, too, one syllable, low:

prayerful, bovine. Mo asks her brother, *do you have a girlfriend yet?*

She leads, spins him around: I love her in a way I couldn't back then.

As a child, I loved the middle girl, Jan, the jealous one, Eve Plumb,

Bible spondee fruit, with a TV J-name, and that blue crochet vest.

When I was a child, I spake as a child, I understood as a child.

When I was a child, I'd see Mo's face on my tin lunchbox, but now I see

her freckles mirrored a small star cluster visible on clear nights—

Constellation of Bejewelled Silver Studs on Soft Velvet Bell Bottoms.

Constellation of Kindness. Constellation of Purple Devotion.

Blades

By a field up past Stowe, I prayed at the edge of an acre of new-
mown hay. When I opened my eyes (having finished my list), I saw
thin black and gold striped snakes

crawling along the tops of the shorn blades:
I thought, *how light and scared they must be to move on those tips*
as they slithered toward the low sun

away from me, searching for darkness and undergrowth.
The whole field moved toward sundown and I almost forgot
how much I feared snakes.

So that's what comes from praying. Long ago,

I sobered up, more than half my life has been spent on the tip of that blade,
bending as far as I can from the point. I am in awe of you,

there with your chunky cut glass of rye, sipping one amber eyelash
at a time. Here, in this pub below the sidewalk, the wood is old oak,
like a man, and dark. The walls are cool brick, brass

weapons hang: crossed blades, a shield like the sun.

Notes

"Is there anything under that layer?" is a quote from Polish artist, Eva Juskiewicz.

"400 Calories of Existential Horror" was a Twitter meme from Boogie2988.

"The Lens" contains a line from Sylvia Plath's "The Bee Meeting."

Ana Mendieta (November 18, 1948 – September 8, 1985) was a Cuban-American performance artist, sculptor, painter who is best known for her "earth-body" artwork. She is considered one of the most influential Cuban-American artists of the post-World War II era. Ana died on September 8, 1985, in New York City, after falling from her 34th-floor apartment in Greenwich Village, where she lived with her husband, the sculptor, Carl Andre. He was acquitted of second-degree murder after a three-year trial in 1988. The acquittal caused an uproar among feminists in the art world, and remains controversial. In 2010, a symposium called Where Is Ana Mendieta? was held at New York University to commemorate the 25th anniversary of her death.

"Yesterday, I Dug All My Sadnesses Out of Their Storage Boxes and Bought a New Pair of Sandals, and Today It Snowed" is a misreading of a Facebook post, which read, "Yesterday, I dug all my *sundresses* out of their storage boxes . . ."

"One Year After My Friend Posted a Photo of Jean-Léon Gérôme's *The Bacchante: Head of a Woman With the Horns of a Ram*," In March, 2021, Samantha Hartsoe discovered an entire apartment accessible through a hole behind her bathroom mirror in her Roosevelt Island apartment.

"The Coleus on Good Friday," contains a line from Rachel Mennies' poem, "April 18, 2017."

"*Bysedd y cŵn,* Foxglove," Life House, or *Ty Bywyd,* is a retreat house, designed by John Pawson, in Wales, near Llanbister. This retreat house, complete with a contemplation chamber for meditation, was used as the setting for the horror movies, *The Feast* and *You Should Have Left.*

"Oloid" is a shape discovered by sculptor and mathematician, Paul Schatz, in 1929. The artist, Julie Chen, explores this shape in her piece, "Chrysalis," which "is an interpretation of the complex and transformative nature of the process of grief." www.flyingfishpress.com

"Did it take long to find me?" This is a line from "Moonshadow" by Yusuf Islam (Cat Stevens)

"Listening to Nicolle Wallace and Thinking of Jericho Brown's Poem," takes its last line from the poem "Night Shift" by Jericho Brown, published in *The New Yorker,* April 9, 2018.

"The Chain" contains a line from Sylvia Plath's, "The Swarm."

"I Find Relationships Exhausting," from an April 19, 2021 *New York Times* article, "There's a Name for the Blah You're Feeling: It's Called Languishing."

"Rilke" refers to Rainer Maria Rilke's poem, "The Man Watching."

Some of my poems were inspired by work presented in my ekphrastic writing group. Much love to all the poets I've met here, especially Laurel Benjamin, who has gathered us.

"Is there anything under that layer?," Eva Juskiewicz, *Untitled, after Èlizabeth Louise Vigée Le Brun,* (Poland, 1984)

"Ceruse," Kay Sekimuchi, *Eleven Leaf* (USA, 2021)

"Rooms," Johannes Vermeer, *Girls at the Open Window* (Netherlands, 1657-8)

"My Friend Can Grow Anything," Emi Uchinda, *Trace,* (Japan, 2018)

"Oloid," Julie Chen, *Chrysalis,* (USA, 2014)

"The Hunter," Alma Woodsey Thomas, *Orion (Space Painting Series)* (USA, 1973)

"The Chain," Edith Rimmington, *Family Tree* (England, 1938)

"Bible Bread," Elena Shlegl, *Hanging Gardens* (Belarus, contemporary)

"Someday, I Shall Love Emily Dickinson's Poems," *Barbara Morgan, Martha Graham 'Celebration (Trio)'* (USA, 1937)

"Blur," Christina Fernandez, *La Vanderia #2* (USA, contemporary)

"Rilke," "A table laid with patterned glass dishes and cups" (USA) 1956 - photo by Chaloner Woods, Getty Images

Acknowledgements

The Academy of American Poets, *Poem-a-Day*, "Corinthians, 13:11"

Anti-Heroin Chic, "American Anemone," "Sandy's Electric Griddle"

Arcturus (The Chicago Review of Books), "Yesterday, I Dug All My Sadnesses Out of Their Storage Boxes and Wore Sandals, and Today It Snowed"

ArtsFuse, "The Chain"

Atticus Review, "The Coleus on Good Friday"

The Bear Review, "Sobriety"

Birdcoat Quarterly, "Luna Maria"

The Bitter Oleander, "Contemplating Vegetarianism"

The Coop: A Poetry Collective, "Hot Things to Me Are Not Dark"

Cream City Review, "I Crocheted a Uterus, But Not Because I Tried" (published as "Confessional Box")

Cutthroat, "Blades," "Listening to Nicolle Wallace and Thinking of Jericho Brown's Poem," "Raising My Son in the Time of Pence"

The DMQ Review, "I Hear About Couples While Stuck on the Massachusetts Turnpike," "Growing Out My Bangs," "The Way This Acela Train/Eats"

Folio, "Is there anything under that layer?"

The Fourth River, "Stone-colored Birds"

Hanging Loose Journal, "I Find Relationships Exhausting"

Hare Review, "The Love of Trees is an Adult Love"

Heavy Feather Review, "Night Snake"

Heron Tree, "Possum Haibun"

The Indianapolis Review, "Did it take long to find me?"

Lily Poetry Review, "Fascism"

Menacing Hedge, "Psychic Party Under the Bottle Tree"

Moria, "Watching a Re-enactment of Dick Cheney's Heart Transplant," "Cremains"

Naugatuck River Review, "Lunaria," (semi-finalist, Narrative Poetry Award)

Nixes Mate Press, "Bryant Park Farmers' Market"

Nelle, "Vision Test in the First Grade"

Pangyrus, "The Drop Off"

Persimmon Tree, "The Structure of Milk"

Phantom Drift, "August"

Plume, "Oloid"

Poetry, "Moon Jellyfish"

Presence, A Journal of Catholic Poetry, "I Address My Catho-alcoholism"

Psaltery & Lyre, "St. Cocaine of Lines, St. Anisette, St. Marijuana, St. Horse," "Waiting for My Son at Midnight by the Church at the Edge of the Small Woods Where the Kids Get Stoned"

River Mouth Review, "Bysedd y cŵn, Foxglove"

Sheila-Na-Gig, "Dr. Martens 1460 Wild Botanica"

The Superstition Review, "O" (published as "Yomi")

The Sonora Review, "400 Calories of Existential Horror"

Talking Writing Magazine, "One Year After My Friend Posted a Photo of Jean-Léon Gérôme's The Bacchante: Head of a Woman With the Horns of a Ram"

Topology, "Phoebe"

UCity Review, "Dear Tortoiseshell Bowl I Stole," "Meat," "Snakes"

The Water-Stone Review, "The Hunter"

Wicked Banshee, "Tarot in a Nicotine Dream"

"The Memory Floor" was printed as a broadside by Nixes Mate Publishers.

"Metamorphosis" was included in the anthology, *Dead of Winter, II*, from Milk and Cake Press

"Sobriety" was included in the anthology, *Without a Doubt*, from NYQ Books.

Love and gratitude to so many people.

All those rooms, my sponsor and my beloved friends who have allowed me to recover. And to those who have passed. In the words of Sandy T., "We are always moving forward."

Eileen Cleary, for your constant and brilliant friendship and your critical eye.

My brilliant friends who brought this book into its shape: January Gill O'Neal, Cindy Veach, Jennifer Jean, Kathleen Aguero, MP Carver, Kali Lightfoot, Richard Hoffman, Clay Ventre, Kevin Carey, J.D. Scrimgeour, Dawn Paul, Colleen Michaels, Barbara O'Dair, Subhaga Crystal Bacon, Brandel France De Bravo, Carla Panciera, Rebecca Olander, KT Landon, Frances Donovan, Anna V.Q. Ross, Sarah Dickinson Snyder, Josette Akresh-Gonzales, Julia Lisella, Erica Charis-Molling.

The Thursday Poets, The Southbank Group, The Good Harbor Poets!

Kelli Russel Agodon, Susan Rich, January Gill O'Neal, and Diane Seuss, for that life-changing workshop when we were all still zooming.

To Vin: forever grateful and in love. And to Mia and Michael, whose art inspires me daily.

And my sisters, Joanie and Liz. Love you always.

About the author

Jennifer Martelli is the author of *The Queen of Queens*, named a "Must Read" by the Massachusetts Center for the Book and winner of the Italian American Studies Association Book Award, and *My Tarantella*, also named a "Must Read," and chosen a finalist for the Housatonic Book Award. She is the author of the chapbooks *All Things are Born to Change Their Shapes*, *In the Year of Ferraro*, and *After Bird*. Her work has appeared in The Academy of American Poets *Poem-a-Day, Poetry, Plume, The Tahoma Literary Review, Scoundrel Time, Verse Daily, Iron Horse Review,* and elsewhere. Martelli has received fellowships from the Massachusetts Cultural Council and The Virginia Center for the Creative Arts.   www.jennmartelli.com